Conscience Outsourced

Does 'not illegal' mean it's OK?

David Harris

immortalise

Acknowledgements.

I acknowledge the input of many people in my friendship communities and beyond who have given me the opportunity to view through their eyes the topics which make up this book.

My immediate support group has supplied invaluable advice, commentary and support:

> Valerie Volk: Adviser, consultant, editor, commentator and divider of wheat from chaff.
>
> Sandra Ramini: Much loved sister, bringing in a lifetime's experience in international journalism.
>
> Mark Worthing. A broad range of skills from theology through to creative writing and editing.

This book would not have been possible without the ongoing support of my *Lebensfährerin* – my fellow traveller in life, Valerie Volk. She has my love, respect and thanks.

The cover illustration.

In ancient Egypt, on death a person's conscience was examined by the god Anubis with a set of scales. They believed that the conscience was in the heart, and murals from tombs show Anubis weighing the heart against a feather. A clear conscience, they believed, would lead to a light heart, which would be outweighed by the feather, clearing the way for the first step to a happy afterlife. In this book we weigh the conscience against the law.

Cover Design: Peter Pollock.

Contents.

Chapter 1 – Whither Democracy?

Signs.

In the euphoria and global emotion at the end of World War II there was a surge in the number of countries setting up democratic systems of government. In 1945 around 500 million people lived under formal democracies. By 2018 that figure was nearer 5 billion, a ten-fold increase.[1] We see democracy as the fairest and most desirable system of government so this is surely a great step forward for humanity.

Churchill assured us that 'democracy is the worst form of government, except for all the others'. In the grand scheme of things it continues to be the least worst because, unlike others, it provides and protects the opportunity for citizens, at regular intervals, to elect a government which will implement their wishes. Interestingly, despite experience, voters are inclined to believe politicians when they are not in power and cast their votes to elect people who they believe will behave honourably in generating and implementing a national conscience[2].

So why is it that in 2021 the world is reeling from the decay of trust, honour, morality and conscience so widespread globally and exemplified by leaders like Erdogan in Turkey,

[1] MaxRange RegimeData 2019 (Many factors at work including break-up of empires)
[2] This does assume rational behaviour, but that's a discussion for another chapter.

Putin in Russia, and that which was very recently on full display in the USA, under President Trump?

Every nation develops a national conscience – a set of principles which guides its actions. The national conscience is an amalgam, a rather messy outcome of the grinding together of the consciences and beliefs of the individual representatives. Everyone in the nation also has a personal conscience. The democratic process gives them the opportunity to allow their conscience to guide them in selecting from the range of candidates on offer at regular elections. It is a great system in concept, but only works if its elected candidates behave honourably. If they do not, there is no reason to expect a democracy to behave any better than an authoritarian government.

In setting, developing and evolving the national conscience the government makes laws. It seems axiomatic that any law passed by the Parliament should be designed to do good for the nation – for everyone – whether they voted for the elected government or not. So, when examining a law it should always be possible to trace the intended implementation of something 'good' back to its beginning, and this 'good' should not be biased towards specific groups within the community at the expense of others.

'Outsourcing' implies letting someone else do some task which you do not want to do, or cannot do, for yourself.

Chapter 1 – Whither Democracy?

Outsourcing is accepted and wide-spread, particularly in the business world, where there are many activities which we know must be done, but which are outside the scope of the individual. To implement schools, police forces, infrastructure construction, we elect governments and pay them, through taxes, to do these tasks. Regular elections provide a feedback process for us to express our approval or disapproval for the way government is performing. This feedback loop is a core strength of democracy.

In a well-functioning democracy all individuals conduct their lives in accord with their own conscience, to the extent that they can, and outsource to the national conscience those things which require the collective wealth and power of the community to achieve. If the government is seen to be operating fairly and honourably, most people will be happy to live their lives within the laws generated and implemented by the government. On these issues, their conscience has been happily outsourced to the law.

But what if government is not acting honourably?

Loss of honour.

Honour. What a quaint, old-fashioned idea, carrying with it ideas of unselfishness, morality, respect, guardianship of the community – even courage. All are ideas which we happily sacrifice on the altar of selfishness, greed and 'business'.

Honour and conscience are closely linked. Conscience is our internal set of morals and principles for living. Honour is our behaviour which demonstrates these morals in use and which shows respect for others.

Today we are seeing a loss of conscience – loss of the still, small voice that says 'is what you are proposing right?' And if we know it is not right but it is profitable, what do we do? Too often it seems that the measure of what is 'right' replaced by the question, 'Is it lawful?' In doing this, we are handing over to the law, issues which should be resolved within our conscience. We outsource our conscience to the law. However, in doing this we have lost something important.

While conscience reflects moral values, the law does not – it is amoral. If we contemplate doing something 'bad', contrary to the moral values encapsulated in our conscience, we are aware of it. We simply *know* it is bad. However, in the national conscience, an action is either in accord with a law or it is contrary to a law. It is either legal or illegal. There is no moral test. But this brings in a further option – what if there is no law affecting our action? There is now a third option: *not illegal*.

Chapter 1 – Whither Democracy?

An example:

A Royal Commission into the banking and insurance industry found that an insurance company was charging life insurance premiums to people who had died. An air of disbelief was registered around the courtroom. We now find that this was global common practice. There is no law to say they could not do this. Who, after all, (with a conscience) would have thought that such a law would be necessary? So it is not illegal, although it is clearly unconscionable.

By *unconscionable* we mean not in accord with conscience. Not in accord with what the typical person in the community would see as fitting comfortably with their conscience. Not in accord with understandings of morality. Not ethical. How does this happen?

If such behaviour is not to occur it requires someone in authority to recognise that the proposal to take this action, while it may be profitable for business, is not in the interests of customers or the community and is therefore unconscionable. Or, to spell it out – dishonourable.

And if this person has sufficient authority to be able to avoid taking dishonourable actions and know that they will not be over-ruled by anyone, then the proposed action would not be done.

It is honour that drives a person to go against their own primal instincts, against their own vested interests, against company profitability and take an action which is in the best interests of their community. We expect, we hope, that our politicians do this every day. Consequently if we see a politician not behaving honourably we expect them to be disciplined. Today, often we expect in vain.

Loss of trust.

If people are honourable, we feel that we can *trust* them to do the right thing. We can expect that, when we hear their words and then observe their actions, we can see that the actions are in the spirit of the words. There will be no weasel words allowing some dubious explanation of a clearly unconscionable action by a warped or laboured interpretation of the words spoken. There will be no 'non-core promises'.[3]

Where there have been no promises made, but a dubious action is proposed, we can expect that the honourable person can be trusted to act in a way which is in accord with the national conscience.

Where there is no law in place the option of 'unconscionable but not illegal' would not be used. The

[3] An invention of former Australian Prime Minister, the honourable John Howard.

honourable action goes further than the national conscience. It uses personal honour to draw on personal conscience, acting as though a law had been implemented to affect the proposed action.

Of course trust, and its antonym treachery, have always been tools of diplomacy. Sun Tsu stated 2,500 years ago that winning by treachery was preferable to winning by battle. The feint – signalling a move and then doing its opposite – is designed to put an opponent off guard, allowing exposed weakness to be exploited. Sadly, treachery is a very effective weapon. However, it has no place in an honour system. Treachery requires the putting forth of a lie, encouraging an opponent to believe it – to trust – and then betraying that trust when it is offered. When treachery is discovered it destroys trust and makes impossible future relationships which would require it. The kind of collaborative relationships upon which a safe, productive and comfortable community relies cannot survive in such a climate. A loss of trust and loss of honour go hand in hand.

In the Nazi regime of the 1930s and 40s Joseph Goebbels effectively turned the idea of trust upon its head, developing methods of maintaining power while abandoning any connection with truth, honour or conscience. Today we still find those who hanker after Goebbels, seeing in his methods valuable lessons in gaining and retaining power over individuals and populations. Thousands of work-years of research in applied psychology in the amoral world of academic study have developed a formidable arsenal of tools for control. Findings have been used for good – for instance getting populations to follow expert advice during a pandemic – but they also find an everyday use in more dubious activities. The world of advertising, recognising that people are rarely motivated by logic, has found other means to fuel consumption. Advertisements use this research to steer a line between truth, deception and greed, and this is on display every day. Where there is no connection to truth this rates as fake news, otherwise known as bullshit, upon which academic treatises have been written.

The revolution in information technology has supercharged this trend. Information in the form of text, pictures, and sound-bites can be spread around the world within minutes without the need to contain any truth at all. In fact, a few truths – enough to provide a measure of credibility – can be wrapped into a believable, but false, story. Attempts to negate such propaganda using truth are ineffective. Facts cannot compete with emotions. We have developed this into a toxic environment in which it is hard to trust anything we see, read or hear. Yet trust, in business and politics, is essential for the function of democracy. The pillars of our civilisation are becoming riddled with termites.

Ratchet.

The use of modern techniques of influence means that, regardless of facts, regardless of publicly available evidence, regardless of personal experience, people can be convinced to believe that activities which clearly degrade their living conditions are for their own benefit. The case of Trumpism and Trump policies in the USA is so obvious that it cannot be ignored. A good example here is health care.

US President Barak Obama brought in universal health care – dubbed Obamacare. Trump spent his time in office unravelling as far as possible every Obama initiative, regardless of its value to society. Yet his political base continued to support him. The result is that people at the low end of the wealth spectrum, people who cannot afford any health insurance, people who can be bankrupted by a health emergency, still support Trump – in large numbers. The recent American presidential election was won comfortably, but not overwhelmingly, by Trump's opposition. Yet many people, including those at the low end of the wealth spectrum, those who could not begin to afford health insurance, who would benefit in large numbers from a universal health care system, continued to support Trump – in their millions.

When something is set in place as a community belief, as is opposition to Obamacare in the USA, it becomes difficult for a subsequent government to remove it. Within pressures to move to the political right, as in the case for the killing of Obamacare (supported by the health insurance industry) there are very strong forces, with very deep pockets and great persistence pushing in this direction. For a move to the political left, the main forces are people power. There is strength in numbers, but the masses have to be rallied, organised and most importantly, funded. That is where well-meaning thinking comes unstuck. It is hard to get a persistent push resourced and hard to maintain it against seriously resourced opposition.

There is, potentially, a more powerful force opposing the right-moving ratchet. It could be formed by a number of honourable politicians. The number would not have to be great. No political party could afford to lose their votes. Their position may be unpleasant, but it is powerful. It is hard to see how this could be formed within a political party. The party Whip would see to that. But independent, unaligned politicians could do it. It is interesting that such unaligned people are being increasingly elected to parliaments in the democratic world. The voting public can be deceived, but not all of them, and not all the time.

Chapter 1 – Whither Democracy?

This imbalance of power in moving the national conscience is most prevalent in those countries where wealth is excessively celebrated, where the focus is on winning. As a result of strong pressures from the right and weaker pressures from the left, there is a kind of ratchet in these countries, creeping notch by notch to the right.

At the extreme right we find Fascism. This is government by an unelected and powerful elite, usually enforced by strong-arm tactics. Memories of avowed fascist governments in Spain, Italy and Germany are receding as those holding the memories enter their 80s and beyond. There are, however, many governments around the world today which, in practical terms, are functionally fascist. Signs of this are the election of presidents for life, elimination of voting or corruption of voting systems so that they become meaningless, brutal crack-downs on opposition, suppression of minority groups and extreme nationalism.

Life under such a government is rarely pleasant.

Chapter 2 – Right and Wrong.

Basics.

The questioning into the concepts of right and wrong goes back into earliest recorded history and no doubt many millennia before. Humans are social beings. We like to live in communities and have been developing ways to do this harmoniously over eons. What most people see as right is something which will be good for our community. Things which are wrong are bad, causing discord or bringing danger to the community. Intrinsic within these concepts are ideas of fairness and unfairness, truth and honesty.

There appear to be two steps in establishing good.

Basic good. Seeking the approval of my community members. This is hard wired in humans as a group-living species.

Cultural action. What the norms are in my community which I need to observe to achieve this basic good. This is learned, and is different (often very different) between communities.

The actions required to meet the basic needs within any culture are culturally determined. They are preserved in the stories of the elders. They are reinforced in music, dance and ceremony (and today in books, films, television, theatre, social media), and are deeply ingrained in every member of the society. Each good in the society is a combination of a cultural action plus the basic need that it satisfies. It is at this level that they exist in the conscience.

Chapter 2 – Right and Wrong.

We recognise that the basic needs of humanity are built into the DNA of all humans, but what a society sees as a good is a culturally determined thing. In our investigations here we confine our attention to what is seen as good and bad within a Western-style democracy. Of course, this implies that our ideals may not be applicable elsewhere, a fact which we need to take on board as our activities become more globalised.

Religion.

Religious beliefs are an integral part of human society. One function of these beliefs is to help define behaviour which is right or wrong in this society. Religion includes (among other things) an amalgam of tribal ancestral stories, understandings of desirable behaviour, rituals reinforcing these beliefs and acceptance and acknowledgement by members of the society that they subscribe to their religion.

Members of a modern, secular society may profess no religion, but we still run our societies on the bedrock of old religious beliefs. We may shrug off the old gods and laugh at their apparently pointless rituals but they still play a significant role in our society, a role recognised, for example, in the laws of freedom of religion.

So, what did religion provide to developing societies? In a dangerous and complex world it provided hope and comfort. It provided a set of moral principles which, if observed, would bring praise and acceptance from peers and their support in life's perils.

There have been as many sets of rules, understandings of good and bad, as there have been human societies. It happens that during centuries of the birth, evolution and growth of the Western style of democracy the Christian church was a powerful and ubiquitous influence. Initially the church was, in effect, the holder of the national conscience, defining right and wrong in its own terms and then teaching it back to the people. However, as societies developed, it became clear that there needed to be a separation between the religious and the secular, between church and state. In increasingly taking over lawmaking, the state began to take on some of the national conscience role of the church until today it has that role entirely – subject, of course, to the democratic will of the people. Churches still make rules which affect their own people but which do not affect the general population except, perhaps by the round-about but acceptable route of affecting votes.

Modern western democracy had its early implementation and development in western Europe, which was, at the time, almost universally Christian. Perhaps the most significant thing which Christianity has contributed to our laws is a concept of fairness in the operation of our society. It was expressed in the Gospels as a command:

Chapter 2 – Right and Wrong.

Love your neighbours and treat them as you would like them to treat you.

The word 'neighbours' was broadened to cover all of humanity, irrespective of nationality, tribe, colour, religion, language, or gender – including enemies.

In practice.

As parliaments were formed it became clear that the behaviour of the elected representatives needed to be honourable, truthful and collaborative. Rules of parliamentary behaviour have been developed over time to encourage this. Similarly, the beginnings of the legal system recognised that, if such laws were to implement the national conscience, they needed careful development of the methods and procedures involved in enacting them. It is also important that, if a law is to be observed, it will need to be policed. Laws must be written in a way to support this.

Today, parliaments have taken on the role of national conscience to which our collective consciences have been out-sourced. It is the generator and controller of what the populace, through the mechanism of democracy, sees as right and wrong.

The influence of Christianity on this process has included the concept of fairness, which is expressed in truth and honest dealing. It provides a basis for evaluating humanitarian issues and is still just as valid today in such areas as human rights. If we would like to be treated with honesty, respect and understanding by others it requires us to behave the same way. It sets a basic idea which allows us, by contemplation of the effects of any proposed action, to decide if that action is right or wrong.

This does not imply that Christianity is a necessary condition for the source of these values. Other religions have similar teachings, which is important as nations become more multi-cultural. But at the time that European democracy was in development, Christianity was the dominant influence.

Tribalism lives.

Within the large societies which make up western democracies, ideas of right and wrong are by no means universal. There are many tribes[4], and what may seem right to one will not necessarily seem right to another. This is the motivation behind the formation of political parties, each representing different world views, different views of right and wrong.

On would hope, and indeed our democratic system is supposed to ensure, that once a parliament of mixed tribal

[4] The word 'tribe' here is used to mean a sub-group of society united by some common belief – a tribal marker. This may be a religion, a language, an economic philosophy, supporters of a football team, etc.

representation is formed it will govern for the good of the whole nation, including those who did not vote for the government. The protocols of the operation of parliament which have been developed over centuries include codes of behaviour which are supposed to encourage fair behaviour, though admittedly in recent decades the observance of these conventions is becoming less evident. Depending on which political group holds sway in parliament, increasing bias can be seen in the laws passed. Think of tax cuts whose announced purpose is to 'increase wages and cut unemployment'. There is voluminous evidence to show that tax cuts have never achieved these goals wherever they have been implemented. As the proposers of this law cannot be unaware of the evidence, the problem being addressed cannot be the one declared but rather the un-declared problem – of a different tribe – of insufficient profit.

Where are we today?

Our internal conscience has its internal understanding of morality and is infinite in its scope. This internal conscience influences us in our choice of candidates to vote for.

Our national conscience pulls together the consciences of the voters, using argument and debate in the parliament.

The parliament then attempts to put the will of the voters into effect, using the limited tool of the law.

So should we get upset about outsourcing our conscience(s) to the parliament/law system if that's the way it's supposed to be? Yes, we should. A myriad of cross-currents affect every twist and turn of life. It assumes, for example, that politicians will behave honestly, collaboratively and honourably. It also places on the table the change from right and wrong to legal, illegal and not illegal. As this last one is often read as unconscionable but not illegal, it is a landmine in the path to truth.

If we could see a parliament in which issues that we care about were argued logically, based on evidence, with respect for both sides, we could be content. If we could see parliament identify real problems, call for reports which would actually identify the issues, and then take note of these reports, we could accept that the system is working. And if it is working, it would lead to the drafting of laws which would take action to address problems and ameliorate them. We would need to see that the proposed laws address the actual problem and not another, hidden agenda, perhaps favouring one 'tribe' and unfairly disadvantaging another.

So, the purpose of this chapter on right and wrong is to outline the progression from something we see as right within our conscience to the implementation of action to make our world a better place, within the bounds of feasibility for the country. It should also identify snags, diversions, ambushes and attacks which one can expect along the way.

We see that we now have two ways to arrive at an understanding of whether something we want to do is good or bad.

The Conscience system, based on our internal conscience:

- If we propose to take an action we examine our proposed action to see if it complies with the culturally accepted ideas of right. If it cannot be shown that it does so comply, then the idea will be abandoned, or it will be modified to make it compliant. The move from idea to action must, necessarily, be passed through a compliance process in accord with conscience.

The Law system, based on parliament + law:

- If we propose to take an action we seek a law which affects it.

  Then …

  - If no law can be found to forbid the proposed action, it is ruled 'not illegal'. Today, this is taken to mean that the proposed action can be done, even if an examination of conscience found it wanting.

19

- If a law is found to forbid the proposed action, then …

  - The proposal will be abandoned, or

  - The proposal will be modified to avoid the sanctions of the law, or

  - The proposal will be continued with anyway, on the assumption that doing it will be more profitable than the consequences of being caught.

It is clear that good and legal are similar. This rests on the assumption that the law was enacted to achieve something of value to the community. Similarly, illegal and bad are similar. However, we have now entered a new concept of 'not illegal' meaning not forbidden by any current law. This can be interpreted in two stages:

> There has so far not been seen to be a need to prohibit this activity in law, and so…

> The proposed activity is not prohibited, and may therefore be done.

In the Conscience system, there is a culturally accepted system of checking that a proposed action is, or is not, in accord with the accepted spirit of the command.

The Law system has no part to play in providing a good/bad valuation. Bad – unconscionable – things can be done if there is no law to prevent them and there will be no sanction in the law. With the powerful in a position to influence the writing of laws, a path is opened for potential corruption.

Chapter 3 – Parliament.

Democracies are built to slow you down. This is useful when those in power want to do despotic things. But it hinders when politicians have the right ideas for the betterment of their people. Autocracies are built for speed. They work brilliantly when those in power are making the right choices (Singapore, the Asian tigers, China during 1980s). They end up in disaster when the direction taken is wrong (Zimbabwe, Russia, Uganda)[5].

Conscience Outsourced is written from within the Anglophone world. The five major countries in this world[6] have inherited centuries of experience from England's history at the time that it was the centre of development of modern mercantile economies. These countries are parliamentary democracies with universal suffrage. Today, western-style democracy is firmly established throughout western Europe and the Anglosphere while many other countries, in search of its benefits, are building and developing their own equivalents.

Key to democracy is the parliament. As we have discussed, it is imperative that, for democracy to work, the parliament must be respected and be worthy of respect. It is the conscience of the nation and must fairly represent the individual consciences of the people, with elected members

[5] R Jagannathan, Times of India. 15/Aug/2019
[6] The UK, USA, Canada, Australia, New Zealand. The largest country in which English is a lingua franca is India, also a democracy and inheritor of British law. The situation is similar for a number of smaller countries which were within the British Empire.

shedding their individual biases to enter into a collaborative theatre of work. This is a big ask and has been recognised as such since Plato who, 3,500 years ago, proposed a 30 year training program with a rigid evaluation process to find appropriate 'philosopher kings'.

We still adhere to Churchill's dictum, that democracy is our best option, so our aim is to preserve and enhance democracy. But we need to have a parliament to which we can confidently outsource the future of our countries. The parliament has built into its operation procedures which attempt to ensure honourable behaviour. There is a chairperson who is in charge of debate. Rules of debate ensure that all members have a chance to be heard fairly. Members are addressed as 'the honourable member' (although this nod to respectful behaviour does not guarantee that that will follow). Codes of conduct exist for members and ministers to minimise conflicts of interest and opportunities for bribery. If these rules are adequately policed they can be effective. Experience today shows that, so much has parliamentary decorum declined that they can be ignored with impunity.

Nation serving.

Governments are given control of the nation's assets and are charged with using them to the best effect for the people of the nation. The operation and administration of the nation, to do the bidding of parliament, is the business of the public service. Although nations have developed into entities of incredible complexity they still have their roots in the old sets of rules of the conscience. Governments are given access to the best expertise and use it to optimise the actions of the nation. This should be done in the best interests of all of its inhabitants, but with the complexity has come a heterogenous population with differing views of the world. No longer is the reason for a rule, or law, obvious. Now a proposed new rule can be – usually is – seen as 'good' by some, 'bad' by others. The government is charged with finding the balance which is best for the nation as a whole.

The conscience of the tribal group reflects its culture. Similarly, today's nations reflect their governments. As the CEO sets the culture of the business, so the government sets the culture of the country. In this way, the nation's conscience is on display. Sometimes with discomfort.

Integrity.

The cynic may feel that, in judging any proposed political action, we can apply three questions:

1. Does it enrich and empower the already rich and powerful?

2. Does it impoverish and weaken the already poor and weak?

3.   Can it be dressed up and presented as a benefit to those it will damage?

If Question 1 brings a 'yes', then it is likely to go ahead.

If Questions 1 and 2 bring a 'yes', then it is almost certain to go ahead.

If Questions 1,2 and 3 bring a 'yes', then it is a shoo-in.

We say that we want our politicians to behave with integrity. What do we mean? The word is defined as:

'Soundness of moral principle and character; uprightness; honesty'.

Even this definition has in it some vague words:

'Moral; Relating to or concerned with right conduct or the distinction between right and wrong.'

We have already looked at right and wrong, showing that they depend on context. We have also shown that, in a heterogeneous society, the same issue can be 'right' for some and 'wrong' for others. In fact, there will be other positions – 'I don't think what they are doing is right, but I see why they are doing it,' and this is before we consider their modern replacements: 'legal', 'illegal' and 'not illegal'.

So what do these terms mean in a modern social-democratic nation?

It is obvious that a moral law must be seen to be one which benefits the nation as a whole and not simply one section of it to the exclusion of others.

It must be transparent, demonstrating to the people that it is being used honestly to their benefit.

Politicians must have no conflicts of interest in operating the law. They must not employ or give favours to friends or family or constituents (or be seen as doing so).

Politicians must not 'feather their own nests' at the taxpayer's expense.

No politician must attempt to justify a clearly immoral act using the excuse that it is 'not-illegal' or that it is 'in accord with procedures' when these procedures can be shown to be inadequate to prevent immoral behaviour.

Politicians who are seen to act without integrity should be immediately removed from special positions of trust.

In other words, when we say we are looking for integrity in our government we are also saying that we expect to see that government acting in accord with conscience. Yet conscience suppression appears to be widespread in our community.

As religion disappears from modern cultures, and with it the teaching and cultivation of conscience, decisions between competing 'goods' become increasingly the province of parliament as the voice of the people. Today we have in our power forces which could make the future heaven or hell.

Who gets to govern?

'We have the best government money can buy.'[7]

As groups get larger, leaders emerge. They can assert a higher status, demanding support from others, and can gain and defend this position through aggression and force of personality. They can also now make rules which are not constrained by their environment – ordering others to do things for them or claiming the most attractive mates. We see the loosening of the links between conscience and behaviour.

Fast forward to today and we find nations of millions led by governments of a few hundred. These few hundred have access to treasuries filled by taxes on all the people. They build and operate national systems and infrastructures. They provide national security, funding and controlling armed

---

[7] Mark Twain.

forces equipped with a broad array of weaponry; they have police forces to control the people and ensure adherence to the laws, which the government creates. Within democracies the government is elected by the votes of the people. In other systems the members of the government have made their way to the top by other means, but once there the business of running the country still comes down to the great mass of the people doing the bidding of those in control, and paying the government for this service through taxes.

It can be seen that, with the resources available to them the people in the governing group need pay little heed to the guidance of their consciences. Nevertheless, the relics of conscience still play a significant part in the thoughts of the people who vote for them. Fairness, compassion and respect are ignored by governments at their peril.

Electioneering.

How do governments get to be elected? What follows applies mainly to major political parties. Smaller parties do not have the resources to put into simply getting elected. They rely on getting enough votes for their reputation and special interests. The major parties spend millions on the process, drawing on experience, psychology and techniques provided by armies of experts.

Chapter 3 – Parliament.

For a political candidate, getting elected or re-elected often has little to do with the government's policies and nothing to do with rationality. To the extent that it has anything to do with conscience this attention is limited to trying not to offend the collective conscience of the people who are likely to vote for the candidate.

With a combination of indoctrination, grooming, and training in public and press presentation, as well as the support of armies of consultants, advisers and tea-leaf readers, what the public sees is avatars rather than real candidates.

Lying.

In simple terms lying means not telling the truth. The objective is to convince the voter to vote for a politician whom they would not vote for if they knew the truth. However, there are levels of lying used for this purpose:

Lies.

You know the truth but deliberately make a statement which you know to be not true. 'A lie told once is a lie. A lie told 1,000 times is the truth.'[8]

[8] Josef Goebbels, Nazi minister of propaganda.

Half truths.

You know the truth, including its nuances. You select a few facts, enough to establish credibility, and then construct a story linking these facts and omitting others which would contradict your story. You then promote your constructed, but misleading, story.

Falsehood.

A story which you want the voters to hear is constructed, with no reference to any facts.

With the aid of research groups, think tanks, and specialist advisers the understanding of human behaviour which is now available has refined programs of lying and deception to an art form which is regularly on display. Those who wish to lie can attend training programs to help them to do so successfully.

Non-core promises.

A term invented by Australian Prime Minister John Howard when he was asked why no action had been taken on an election promise. He described the promise as a 'non-core promise' which we are expected to read as 'a nice idea, and yes, I promised it, and perhaps I'll get around to it one day when I have time.'

Chapter 3 – Parliament.

Pork barrelling.

Directing money or discriminatory actions towards particular electorates – essentially bribes – to affect the vote for a party's candidate. This technique is usually directed towards marginal electorates, where the vote is likely to be close. The 2019 'Sports Rorts' affair in Australia is a well-documented example[9].

Announcements.

When a government decides to go ahead with a new project it announces it. However, in the run-up to an election we see projects announced which have the aim simply of encouraging voters. There are projects which are 'announced' but which never see the light of day after the election. Projects are announced which are simply a 'thought bubble' which will, with investigation, be found to be impractical or not viable. Old projects will be re-badged and announced as new. There is a complete disconnect between the announcement and the implementation of the project.

Battle lines vs collaboration.

This is encouraged by the press, knowing that conflict gets more 'eyes' than peace and harmony. The press slogan 'if it

[9] Award of Funding under the Community Sport Infrastructure Program. Australian National Audit Office, 15th January, 2020.

bleeds, it leads' is true, and politicians know that any publicity is good publicity. So, denigration of opponents, denigration of the opposition's proposed program, personal mud-slinging are framed into a conflict. The news reports generate more publicity.

Rumour spreading.

Rumours are used by all sides of politics to spread false stories about opposing candidates or their programs. Social media have made possible the spread of such rumours around the world in minutes. There are organisations of fact checkers who take on the task of checking the worst of these rumours. Collecting the relevant facts they report on the validity of the claim made in the rumour. This is helpful to some but rumours live on emotions, not facts. Another action possible today is that rumours can be directed at specific recipient groups. They can be invisible to the public, to the person targeted or to the fact checkers.

In electioneering, conscience is completely thrown out of the window and replaced by emotional manipulation – now an art in itself – feeding from the world of scientific research in psychology and human behaviour.

Law making.

In the modern context the governing body makes the laws. We have seen that, unlike the distant past, there are few natural restraints on what laws can be made. One is reminded of the USA State which passed a law defining π (pi, the ratio of a circle's circumference to its radius) as having the value of 3 instead of its natural (and unalterable) value of 3.14159. But it goes beyond that. Once the law has been enacted, it must be put into effect, which requires funding. The Government has control over the amount of funding it will receive. If the law is in any way contentious it will also need to be policed. This will require the engagement and training of people to police it, funding them and giving them the power they will need to carry out their task. Offences against the law will need to be prosecuted, or if challenged will need to be defended in court. And there is the possibility for conflict of interest between parliamentarians and business.

In the British legal case law system, as cases are tried over time the law is clarified and defined by the findings in these cases. However, the effectiveness of the law can be derailed by actions as simple as de-funding the body concerned with policing.

Chapter 4 – The Law.

The law in the English speaking world is the jewel in the crown, the cornerstone of its culture. It is admired across the globe. In this discussion we are focusing on the use of the law in relation to unconscionable behaviour.

In the system of common law the interpretation of a law is developed and expanded on the basis of cases judged. In this way the law is not static and is capable of adapting to its changing environment. If a law on the statute books is directly relevant to what you are doing, or intend to do, a ruling can be made on whether the action is or is not in accord with the law. It can be ruled 'legal' or 'illegal' and can be tested in a court of law. Even if it may be considered unconscionable it may still be not illegal. Today 'unconscionable but not illegal' is taken as being 'OK to proceed'.

There are many other rules and restraints governing acceptable behaviour including council by-laws, codes of conduct, regulations and accepted practices. Infringement of these can lead to punishments ranging from warnings to a professional being prevented from practising. There is also a very important set of codes of conduct covering the behaviour of politicians, in the parliament and outside. In investigating the behaviour of the law we include all of these restraints together with statute law as a set of behaviour controllers.

The law watered down.

Some laws must strike a very narrow balance. Laws covering gambling, or gaming, are among these. We will take this example and discuss it in some detail as a case study.

Gaming is enjoyed by many. People like a bet and Australians spend over $20 billion a year on gaming, most of it poured into the country's 200,000 poker machines. This national addiction makes the gaming industry a great money-spinner, with the government a prime player, receiving a rich income in taxation. The downside is that gaming soaks up money which could be better spent – 'better' in that this kind of money can put financial hardship on gamblers and their families. In the extreme case of gambling addiction it can be life-wrecking.

So, on the one hand, there is pressure from socially-concerned society, both inside and outside of government who want to see gambling constrained, regulated and, ideally, eliminated. On the other hand, there are those who see gaming as a harmless recreation and object to 'do-gooder' interference. These people, backed and supported by the gaming industry, want to see all restrictions minimised or removed. We can see the effect of this tug-of-war in the world of poker machines.

The operation of poker machines has many detractors. They are seen by many as a social ill, driving the susceptible to addiction and destroying lives. Popular concern has seen candidates elected into parliaments on 'no-pokies policies', working towards the elimination of poker machines.

Yet, many others see the 'pokie lounge'[10] as a pleasant place to 'get lucky' feeding a machine. Poker machines have also been found to be very effective money harvesters, keeping many pubs and clubs financially viable. Governments face a dilemma. On the one hand, they are reluctant to offend their constituents, including small businesses which survive on the income. On the other, they recognise the need to control the poker machines themselves to prevent dishonest behaviour by operators. The machines fall under state jurisdictions and all have facilities for inspecting the machines, measuring their performance, and monitoring their use in the field. Outside these two business issues is the social problem of gambling addiction.

Machine manufacturers have made use of modern psychology research and do everything possible to make the whole experience highly attractive – fun for the average punter, deadly for the potential addict. Machines are attractively decorated, display flashing lights and play

[10] An Australianism. We understand that it may seem amusing to other nations.

jingles to accompany playing and offer soft rewards. They are carefully controlled to make sufficient payouts to keep people playing while ensuring that they are earning the maximum amount permitted under the law. The effect has extended into the environment in which the machines operate, with designer lighting, free coffee and attractive attendants. There are no clocks in casinos. The only time is playing time and they are open all hours of the day and night.

Then there is the 'social ill' argument which has convinced some jurisdictions to ban poker machines[11]. Even where the benefits are seen to be worthwhile they are heavily regulated. Given their potential for harm the uncontrolled and widespread use of poker machines can be considered unconscionable.

The laws and regulations governing poker machines and pokie parlours do come up periodically for review, but there is continual, strong pressure to minimise the effects of these laws which appears to be on the winning side at present. The long hours of operation of pokie parlours and gradually increasing cost per spin show the effect that the designers and operators of these gambling machines have on the law-makers. It is the government which makes the laws so its behaviour in watering-down its own laws and regulations

[11] For example, Western Australia, where they are permitted only in a casino.

contributes to the unconscionable side effects of the machines. Unconscionable, you might say, but not illegal, except that their legality is measured against laws which the government itself has made – a somewhat circular argument.

The law weaponised.

Originating in the military world, the term 'weaponising' originally applied to taking a technology which has a benign origin and developing it to be effective as a weapon. Chlorine gas, which has many benign uses in the chemical industry, was used as a weapon against troops in World War 1. Since then, poisonous gas as a weapon has been developed and refined into a terrifying array of chemical weapons. Gas has been weaponised.

The term 'weaponising' has taken on a wider meaning today, and is now applied to the development and extension of a law to enable it to be used for some purpose other than its original intention. In particular where that new purpose allows it to be used unconscionably. Treatment of whistle-blowers is a good example.

The word 'whistle-blower', coined by journalists in the 1960s, describes a person or group who, acting on their conscience, points out that a government or corporation is acting to prevent information becoming available, information which the public has a right to know. They are

38

acting, in their opinion, to expose unconscionable behaviour. Governments made laws, originally to protect whistle-blowers, recognising that shooting the messenger is unhelpful. However, the actions of whistle blowers were found to be often critical of governments. The reaction of governments was to turn the legislation around so that it now targets them rather than protecting them. Today the legislation has been 'weaponised' against whistle-blowers, sharpening and shaping it, to increase its effectiveness when used to attack. It can now be used to target the news media, setting the resources provided by the state under the law to track down sources of embarrassing news stories.

In a democratic society it is vital for a free press to expose information that others, including and especially governments, do not want exposed. It is also vital that the anonymity of these sources is protected. While there are laws to protect highly sensitive information, the substantive difference between this and the simply embarrassing is understood within the conscience.

An example has to be the totally unconscionable Australian government bugging of the government buildings of the new republic of Timor Leste. For Australia to make a support gesture by constructing the building then to place listening devices in the conference room was bad enough, but then to collect information for, and supply it to, a multi-billion dollar company to assist them in their negotiations for an oil resource under the Timor Sea was unconscionable to the point of jaw-dropping.

So where does the law get involved in this embarrassing saga? The bugging was exposed by a whistle-blower who could not live comfortably with this knowledge and which drove him to expose it. The law was set in motion to prosecute the whistle-blower and, in a further step into a police state, his lawyer as well. The law was extended and toughened to become more punitive, including raiding premises, dragging out proceedings for years, and destroying the lives of both men. This law is now weaponised to a frightening degree.

Justice delayed is justice denied. The operation of the law is, by its nature, slow, despite the old adage justice delayed is justice denied. The collection and verification of evidence is vital to an informed verdict but the law can be manipulated to draw out a trial for years. During all of this time the end result is unsure, causing financial, mental and social harm to complainants. The law here is being used as a weapon to drain the resources – and the will – of the challenger so that the procedure cannot be continued.

Outgunning.

Changes to the law can be initiated in several ways and one of these is objections from communities when their amenity or their livelihood is threatened by proposed actions, especially from large corporations or by government. An example would be objections from a farming community to fracking for gas where they fear that this will poison sweet water aquifers and adversely affect – in fact, destroy – their operations.

The experience of small groups like this when taken up with the government will typically include a meeting with the appropriate minister. The leaders of the group, perhaps with a lawyer, will find themselves confronted in a meeting with the minister they came to meet accompanied by other politicians, heads of several related departments, several executives of the company they are complaining about and a bevy of lawyers from all of the opposing parties.

If a mining company stands to lose access to a multi-million dollar asset it is worth spending all it takes to make their case. It will have far deeper pockets than the complaining group who, confronted by a potentially expensive legal fight, may simply back off. Should they continue the fight, the defending organisation will move into an attack so commonly used that its actions can be ticked off a list as they occur.

They will:

> Use their lawyers to pick over every point put forward in order to argue or contest.

Denigrate the complaining group with attacks on their integrity.

Denigrate any experts the complaining group may have consulted or used, questioning their reputation, skills and motives. This, of course, can be professionally damaging to the expert, making them reluctant to be involved.

Find experts who have opposite opinions. These can always be found.

Take the case to court, spin it out for as long as possible to drain the complaining group, financially and physically.

Lobby hard the government members involved, placing them in invidious positions (your refusal will cost thousands of jobs!)

Of course this could be seen as simply the working of the democratic process. The issue is the power imbalance which allows the use of the law to destroy and exhaust the complainant.

Loopholes.

We have seen that the functions of the law and the conscience in resolving an issue have a fundamental difference in approach. This has been discussed in Chapter 1, on Right and Wrong.

If a law exists which affects the proposed action it has been put in place by the government, presumably, to achieve a 'good' end. It will have been structured to try to achieve this so that upholding the law should produce a good result for the community. Conversely, not upholding the law, quite apart from being illegal, would produce a bad result for the community. It is often possible, through examining the minutiae of the law, to find a way in which the proposed action can be achieved without offending the strict wording of the law. In this way, a 'bad' action which the law was created to prevent, has become possible. This is a classic loophole.

Where such behaviour is contemplated by a member of parliament there will, typically, be Codes of Ministerial Behaviour in place. A typical example may be:

1. A Minister may not discuss with a business operating within his portfolio the possibility of work with the business after retirement.

2. A Minister may not take up employment with such a business within 18 months after retirement.

What is the 'good' which this code of conduct is intended to achieve? In optimising the value of competition and its effective role of the capitalist system it is important that competition should be on a level playing field. All companies competing must have equal access to expertise with no possibility of unfair favour. A minister acting in his portfolio will have close and detailed information which will be of value if made available, exclusively, to one business. The Code of Behaviour is intended to avoid such exclusive access while a minister is in position. It then requires an 18 month cooling off period during which the now ex-minister's knowledge and contacts should have diminished to a level not to threaten true competition. So the code has a 'good' purpose.

Let us now surmise that a minister finds himself in a position where he is offered a secure working life after retirement if his knowledge can be made available immediately upon his retirement to one company exclusively.

So, the company has offered to pay the minister for access to his expertise immediately upon his retirement.

It has also suggested a mechanism to achieve this without their employing him directly, thereby avoiding the restraints of the code of ministerial practice. It would help him to join a consulting firm which provides services to a range of customers. The interested firm would then engage these consultants. It is the business of the consulting company which staff member does what. So allocation of staff to particular customers is an internal matter.

The firm has defined a loophole to achieve their aims, getting around the wording of the ministerial code.

The two limitations of the code can be viewed in two ways:

The Law: Looking at the Code of Practice:

1. No discussion. This is easily deniable. If the ex-Minister denies that such a discussion has taken place, he must be believed, or at least given the benefit of the doubt. So, no contravention.

2. No employment. The ex-Minister does not take up employment with the company, but with a consulting company which has many customers. So, no contravention – not illegal.

Conscience: Looking at the purpose of the Code of Practice:

1. No discussion. This is easily deniable. None but the people involved would know the truth, and denial must be given the benefit of the doubt.

2. No employment. This is unconscionable. The loophole around the code means that it is 'not illegal' but it allows behaviour which the Code was intended to prevent.

It is clearly up to the Minister and others involved to modify their behaviour to make it conscionable. Or simply not do it. This would be the honourable approach by the 'honourable' member.

Not solving the problem.

A new law is initiated when a problem in the function of the community requires it. Parliament then drafts a law to address or solve this problem. It is, however, possible to create a law where there is evidence available that it will NOT address the problem.

So when an Australian Prime Minister, addressing the issue of unemployment said he would be taking action to 'create jobs, decrease unemployment and increase wages' he needed to propose a methodology to achieve this. His proposed methodology was to cut corporate taxes. He was asked how this would work, and responded: 'With this tax relief, companies will have money available to employ more workers and pay them more.' When further pressed to point to another country which had done this (of which there are many), and had achieved the results proposed, he was unable to do so. The same question had been put to the Chair of the Australian Manufacturers Association, who was also unable to identify such a country but agreed to 'take the question on notice'. No answer was ever forthcoming. From many examples, there was no country which had been able to show a beneficial effect on unemployment and wages from cutting corporate taxes. Strictly speaking, of course, it only needs one negative result to scuttle the theory.

The Prime Minister was further pressed on the topic and finally responded: 'Well, cutting corporate taxes is good for the economy anyway!' It appears that the 'good' which the PM's action was taken to produce was not the 'good' which he had put forward to the electorate. He went ahead to implement these changes, to no obvious beneficial effect on wages or employment.

So if the evidence from around the world was against the likely success of the proposed action, and if the Prime Minister knew this, why did he continue to implement corporate rate cuts? Of course there were many powerful political currents and cross-currents which made the decision go this way. But it would be nice to think that evidence of effectiveness could play some part in political decisions.

Uncompetitive behaviour.

The creative power of capitalism requires free competition on a level playing field. This forces firms to out-do each other, competing on the basis of their skills and creativity. However, this model carries within itself an antagonism towards competition. The capitalist business model strives for maximum profit for shareholders with drivers of maximum sales income (Income = sales volume x selling price of products) and minimum cost. Competition inevitably involves having to share the market with others. This competitive pressure is one of the strengths of the system, forcing companies to work hard on refining their products. Company boards appear sometimes not to take this constructive view if other options become available.

As company size gets larger there is strong pressure to seek a position of monopoly. With no competition to control selling prices, these can be increased. With no competition to share the marketplace, sales volume can be higher. Reduction of competition can be achieved by driving out competitors or by buying them out. Large size and financial strength is important in both of these strategies.

Government recognises the value of large, strong local companies in benefiting from wealth creation in country. They also provide a high-level business training ground in which the entrepreneurs of tomorrow can develop and hone their skills and spread them into the community.

While governments recognise the value of competition they also recognise the danger of monopoly and make laws to control them. However, government is conflicted. It needs to encourage a multitude of smaller, creative firms to generate and fuel new developments. Larger firms can also feed on these, buying up the more successful and providing greater markets for their products, and gaining strength in the process. But in doing this they are moving towards a monopoly position.

While this argument is appropriate for some businesses it is not so for others, and these others are where the government needs to be directly in control. Obvious examples are the defence forces, law enforcement and health care. The conflict arises from the fact that the delivery of some services must be kept within the reach of all of the population, irrespective of its cost and profitability. An example currently in focus is the provision of aged care in nursing homes. It appears that the provision of this service at a level of quality and safety which the government requires cannot provide profits at levels required by investors. The result has been the rise of private investment groups providing sub-standard care which has led to misery, illness and death.

Governments are elected to pass laws which dictate behaviour to provide benefit to the community, and/or to forbid behaviour which is not in the best interests of the community. The law then takes on some of the role of the conscience, all the more important as the power of the consciences of the people involved becomes ever less able to control behaviour.

Because of these conflicted interests the laws made by the government to control competition need to strike a balance. With the pressures on the government from all sides, the interests of large enterprises often prevail until, as in the case of nursing homes, public anger forces governments to take action. The laws, like any others, once passed by parliament are there for the legal system to implement. Opposition from those adversely affected must be expected. The restraints of the laws will be challenged and the methods outlined above will be used to circumvent them.

The laws must be adequately policed – if they are not it will be realised that they can be ignored. Adequate policing must be properly resourced, and the doer of the policing must be given the power to prosecute. If the government chooses to outsource its desired activities to the private sector it needs an arms-length, disinterested policing force, preferably itself or to an agency which it pays. The reason is that a private company taking on a service of policing or auditing is conflicted. It must examine and report truthfully on the provision of the service the government requires, but at the same time, its duty to its own shareholders is to gain on-going business. If it gets a reputation of being 'hard to get on with' or 'intrusive,' businesses may be reluctant to give it business. To keep its costs down it may turn to doing its investigations by telephone, which is essentially limited to making sure the paperwork is correct when what is needed is random, on-site inspection by people skilled in the field who will notice unreported discrepancies.

Summary.

All of the points made above are not intrinsic to the legal system but the result of the ways the laws are created and supported by the government. The legal system is simply involved in their application. Within the swirling eddies of power, money, economics and politics it is too easy to lose sight of conscience. Within any economy there is rarely any topic which is an absolute 'good'. The mining company drilling for gas sees its contribution to the economy as fundamentally important, but the farmers whose water supplies are vital for survival are convinced that theirs is the cause with 'good' its side.

As the influence of religion diminishes within modern cultures and with it the cultivation of conscience, decisions between competing 'goods' become the province of parliament, as the voice of the people. Today we have in our power forces which could make the future heaven or hell.

Perhaps we should leave the last word to Plato who, 2,500 years ago, laid down primary considerations in the operation of a democracy:

Good people do not need laws to tell them how to act responsibly, while bad people will find a way around the laws.

Chapter 5 – The Business of Business.

Western democracies have a business community which is a mix of private enterprise and government-run enterprises. As a mix it is healthy and necessary as the business model of each is not necessarily appropriate to the other. We will focus on private enterprises.

There have been many criticisms of behaviour across the whole spectrum of business from underpayment of workers, theft of wages, unskilled staffing and providing minimal service to customers. Why is this? Obviously it's about money, about profit and loss. But even when the stakes are high, surely businesses do not set out to behave unconscionably.

A light dose of morality.

The outstanding survival success of the human race has been achieved through our ability to live in cooperative harmony in large groups. At various stages of the evolution of modern society wise people have developed sets of rules to live by. We call them 'moral' codes. They are human-developed and are taught to us in infancy as things we ought to do despite the internal drives we have inherited.

These moral concepts help form the basis of our conscience and have been extended into such ideas as fairness, compassion, humility and respect. These moral values have become, at best, 'nice-to-have' in the amoral business of business.

What is business for?

The capitalist model of business has produced a remarkable range of products and services, affordable by the average person, and much of it beyond the wildest dreams of kings of the past. It has accomplished this by rewarding human effort and creativity, in particular in science and engineering as well as in sales and marketing. It also requires a competitive environment and, as near as is practical, a level playing field. Yet it is also a ruthless environment, reflecting what happens in nature. The clever, imaginative and hard-working succeed against others. Those who perform best rise to the top and when market performance is matched by quality goods and services the winners are not just the customers but the businesses that provide them – a win/win result.

Yet there are many opportunities for behaviours which we may not like. But are they unconscionable? If a wolf picks out the lame sheep from the flock, or the shark the seal pup, is this unconscionable or simply the function of the food chain doing its job of honing the capabilities of the population? Honing the capabilities, incidentally, of both prey and predator.

The competitive model, however, carries within it the seeds of its own degradation. If a large firm is threatened by a competitor it may be encouraged to come up with innovative ideas of its own. This is expected from a competitive, capitalist economy. However, if it has trouble doing this it may scratch the competitive itch by taking action to remove the competitor. We are reminded of the advice of Sun Tsu that it is better to win by treachery than by fighting. If such a large player is able to completely eliminate its competition it achieves a monopoly which introduces major issues of its own.

Competition.

As we have discussed earlier, competition is fundamental to life on earth, including human life. It is a driving force behind evolution, where traits helpful to survival are be passed down by survivors to their offspring. Unhelpful traits disappear. Every living organism has predators and prey. Its survival depends upon it being better at avoiding its predators and being better at catching and consuming its prey. Darwin's 'survival of the fittest' comes to mind. There are no moral issues involved here. Anything that works will be used.

There are behaviours seen in the natural world which humans could do, but are held back by the moral constraints which they hold in their conscience. A leopard, seeing a cheetah dragging away a kill, may threaten it with death or injury and rob it of its meal. We can visualise a similar situation in a human community, but as such behaviour would be antithetical to the harmony of the society it would be unlikely to happen. In fact, if the hunter were to bring such a kill back to the tribe, a desirable behaviour would be to share it.

In a society in which members can be expected to behave in accord with their conscience the above scenario could be expected. However, we see business as amoral – inherently neither moral nor immoral, neither good nor bad. In principle, business can do what it likes, which could lead to the law of the jungle. If we wish to prevent this we must reward moral behaviour, firstly by instilling a conscience in all members of our tribe, and then backing this up with a system of laws which are enforced by the community as a whole. This a clear case of outsourcing our consciences to the law.

This presents us with a dilemma. Previously we could rely on the application of individual conscience to do the best for the tribe. Now, in an amoral business environment, we rely completely on the law and this is where we move from conscientious behaviour to legal behaviour. We replace two options – good and bad with three – legal, illegal and unconscionable-but-not illegal. We do our best to ensure that all bad behaviours are covered by laws which we invent and implement. However, when a new behaviour arises (or is engineered) for which no preventative law exists or where work-arounds or loopholes are discovered, the acceptance of amorality for the business world means that such a behaviour can be carried out with no penalty (and no remorse).

In a competitive business environment we try to set a field of operation in which all businesses have a fair opportunity to thrive – a level playing field. However, if a particular business finds a way to tilt the field in their direction, we see two typical outcomes:

> If the new behaviour is not prevented by law (no matter if it is immoral or unconscionable) then others will copy it. If they do not, they will be at a competitive disadvantage.

> If society sees the new behaviour as unconscionable it should take steps, through its elected government, to make the new behaviour illegal.

We have made the point that, while natural constraints are immutable, human-made laws are just that – made by people. People do not always behave rationally or even fairly.

Wage pressures

Unemployment is seen by governments as an issue to be addressed. Since the flight of major manufacturing industry from rich countries to poorer, developing countries (with a strong push from governments) that industry and its surrounding skirts of competent and efficient manufacturing suppliers is no longer present. Apart from its role in providing the nation with world-class manufacturing industry, it was also a major employer. Manufacturing will still exist but on a smaller scale. There is scope for expansion in low and zero emission industries (in the face of fierce antagonism from fossil fuel lobbies). In some countries, unemployment is soaked up by a growing and strongly government-supported defence industry. However, the most effective focus on providing employment (i.e., reducing unemployment) is in labour-intensive industries such as tourism, hospitality and aged care.

All developed countries have laws governing employment with provisions for fair wages, safety and industrial issues. These vary from country to country and can include a selection of minimum wages for normal working hours, provisions for paid holidays, paid maternity leave, paid long-service leave, penalty loadings for working shifts, nights and holidays. All of these conditions have been hard won over decades. All vary with required skill levels and all apply to actual employees, and not to contractors.

In many jobs people can be replaced, sometimes by technology, sometimes by off-shoring work to low-wage countries. However in the labour-intensive areas mentioned above, the work must be undertaken by people located on the spot. There is continual pressure on the government from these business sectors to 'do something' to lower wages. The code word used is 'flexibility'.

Some illegal methods can be found. Businesses can simply ignore the law and pay below award wages. They are unlikely to be caught as employees are too worried about their jobs to complain and there is little policing. Comments like, 'I didn't know I was under-paying – the system is complicated' or, 'everyone is doing it' litter the workplace with their duplicity. These difficulties seem to be no hindrance in claiming government industry support payments.

Under pressure from business, laws have been created to provide employers with greater flexibility by allowing the hire of contractors rather than employees. In principle, there is nothing wrong with this. A contractor with specialist skills would be put in place to provide the employees, instruct them and train them to carry out work under the instruction of the business. The hiring contractor is expected to provide the employee benefits, charging the business an appropriate amount to allow these costs to be covered. The problem arises when the business hires 'contractors' which are each simply a single person. The laws and protections covering permanent employees no longer apply. No single employee can afford to charge an amount which covers employee benefits, because there will always be someone desperate enough not to insist on it.

This provides many 'not illegal' methods for lowering the amounts paid to these contractors or workers with the added benefit that their jobs are under continual threat. In order to stay afloat this business and all its competitors would be forced to use the same methods for reducing wage costs.

This is unconscionable. Of course, as we have said before, 'unconscionable, but not illegal' becomes 'okay to do'.

Corruption.

Strictly speaking, 'corruption' is doing something illegal for personal gain. It is criminal. However, as 'illegal' means 'against the law' and as the law is human-made and can be changed to make a previously unconscionable and illegal act no longer illegal, but still unconscionable, we will include such acts in our definition of corruption.

Jobs for the boys.

This well-known scenario doesn't need to involve the government but looks worse when it does. For example, a government project comes up, and several experienced companies, expert in this kind of work, tender for it. Yet somehow the work is given to a contractor, who is not best suited to the job but who has clear links to a politician.

To implement a project by outsourcing it a government should follow a process to ensure that it is getting value for money. This includes:

- Drawing up a specification which details exactly what the contractor shall provide.

- Putting out this specification for tender, either publicly or at least to businesses in the area of the proposed work.

- Preparation of proposals by firms interested in taking on the work and submission of these proposals to the department issuing the tender.

- Evaluation of the proposals by the department to ensure that they meet the specification, and to identify areas where it may not be met (which may be negotiable).

- Checking the proposed prices for the work to confirm that they are reasonable in the light of the work needed.

- Carrying out a 'due diligence' check to gain confidence that the firm is likely to be able to carry out the work successfully, both on the basis of past experience and of financial viability.

A successful tender is chosen and this recommendation is provided to the appropriate government minister or official. If the vetting and selection process is valid then, by definition, any other selection must be less beneficial for the country.

If the minister or other official ignores this recommendation and awards the job to a different firm, which may or may not have submitted a proposal, the question must be asked – why has this decision been made? If it is found that the politician concerned has links to the now successful tenderer they are guilty of malpractice, and probably conflict of interest. A job has been given to 'the boys'.

To be found to have done this would, years ago, have led to censure and serious damage to the politician's career. These days, it seems, not so much.

Corporate behaviour.

Where a government contract is put out for the provision of a community service it sees the service as its main priority. The company, however, sees making a profit as its main priority. In an ideal situation, if problems are experienced in providing the service profitably, a solution should be negotiated by the government department with the company. After all, it is not in the government's interest either for the contractor to go out of business or for a sub-standard service to be provided.

There is, however, a strong incentive for the contractor to 'game' the system to meet the strict requirements written into the specification in a way which reduces their costs while providing a reduced and sub-standard service. A good example of this came to light in the private sector during the Hayne Royal Commission into the banks. A particular bank was found to be notorious for foreclosing on farmers and selling up their assets when, if they had waited for a few months for the payment for a crop to be received, the farmer could have paid off the debt. The bank employees were aware of this situation. However their masters ran an incentive scheme for its employees where a bonus was paid on the number of these debt situations which were 'resolved' within a certain time. Employees were encouraged to foreclose to get the required 'runs on the board' to maximise their bonus. The needs of the farmers did not enter into the equation.

Gaming the system is common when a way can be found to downgrade the service, reduce costs and increase profit. Large amounts of lawyers' time is spent finding ways this can be achieved without, technically, breaching the contract. In the Aged Care sector the government did not specify a staff-to-client ratio, partly because it did not want to restrict 'private enterprise business know-how' in providing the service at minimum cost. In practice, these ratios reached levels at which good service could not be provided – a loophole was exploited. The government played its part by supplying minimal resources for policing the regulations and producing little more than a slap on the wrist if any non-compliance was ever discovered.

Update:

At the time of writing (January 2021) a 2-year progress report on the implementation of the Hayne royal commission was published.[12] The report contained 76 recommendations for implementation to overcome the malpractices found. When the original report was handed to the government, two years earlier, the Treasurer promised action on 'all 76 recommendations'.

Two years later the state of play is:

- 27 recommendations have been fully implemented.
- 45 are 'in work'.
- 4 have been abandoned.

The Treasurer reported that '70% of the recommendations have been implemented'. Examination of the fine print shows that 70% of those changes which require changes to the law have been implemented. This is just a sub-set of the 76 Hayne recommendations. The majority of the harmful practices which were revealed in the commission were contrary to existing law anyway so the recommendations were designed to ensure that the companies stopped breaking existing law. As these don't require changes to the law they fall outside the Government's 70%. One should not be so naive as to assume that 70% of the original 76

---

[12] The Guardian, 27/Jan/2021. Presenter Laura Murphy-Oates.

recommendations of the Commission (i.e., 53 recommendations) had been fully implemented.

As the government sorts its way through what to do next, there is a huge effort by the industry to water down the recommendations. The issue, as we point out in Chapter 6, is that what the public seeks is honourable behaviour.

Greed lives in the individual conscience at the hard-wired, basic survival level. It is not accessible to the influence of honour except through the higher, culturally built level of conscience whose purpose is to control those basic urges which are inimical to cooperative behaviour. The findings of the Hayne commission show the degree to which honour has been abandoned, allowing greed to triumph.

Corrupting government.

As we have noted, 'jobs for the boys' requires corrupt behaviour on the part of the government. Why would they do this? Could it be put down to a simple case of 'if you scratch my back I'll scratch yours'?

Obviously it is in the interests of business to make sure that government officials are sympathetic to their cause. The wheels of finance and profit turn more smoothly when a comfortable relationship with a powerful politician or political party is in the background.

Large donations to political parties help ease the way for successful lobbying. It is a continual, unrelenting and well-resourced aspect of big business. With government stretched to do an adequate job of drawing up laws, putting up tenders for work and providing intellectual power in decision-making, friendly offers from business to 'help' with this work can be useful in gaining preferential treatment. Especially when that encouragement includes offers to politicians for employment after retirement or other favours such as travel or donations to favoured causes.

Organised crime.

We have already made the point that activities like the manufacture and provision of alcohol and the manufacture and provision of illicit drugs fall on a continuum. The value of alcohol in providing relaxation and recreation to a large part of the population makes it acceptable to the government. Its potential for damage is recognised and regulations are made to keep this under control. The step over into illicit drugs involves many of the same activities. The difference is defined simply by laws.

The pressures felt by business to modify, avoid or work around the laws are felt in the same way by organised crime, and many of the same techniques are used by both. Where an unconscionable activity has nevertheless a high demand in the community, it is very much in the government's interest to legalise the activity as much at the parliament will allow. It then has at least some oversight and control. If an activity is highly profitable and illegal – as illicit drugs are by definition – then it will attract the attention of criminals. While legal action to enforce laws may be uncomfortable, it is benign in comparison with the enforcement techniques of organised crime.

Corruption of officials can move into threats, blackmail and heavy-handed enforcement. The large sums of money involved facilitate bribery and also allow engagement of the most effective lawyers.

Is it fair to include organised crime in such a review? During the Hayne Royal Commission one of the large banks admitted that it had processed 1.2 million transactions which could have involved money laundering. The animals (i.e., business and organised crime) are so similar in appearance and operation that they are, at times, difficult to tell apart.

Power plays.

We have made the point that power and money are opposite faces of the same coin. The huge amounts of money which flow through large businesses provide the power to take actions to protect them even when their activities are opposed by the government of the sovereign states in which they operate.

Chapter 5 – The Business of Business.

Resisting change.

The tobacco industry is established on the basis that people enjoy using nicotine. Users of this drug are prepared to pay amounts for it which provide large profit margins over the costs of its delivery system – cigarettes. The cost of growing tobacco is low and its use in making cigarettes is simple, especially when done in the enormous quantities consumed around the world. The government is somewhat conflicted by the very high taxes it collects on tobacco, while striving to reduce their use for community health reasons.

The link between cigarette smoking and lung cancer was discovered in the 1920s in Germany. However, attempts to limit its consumption were actively resisted by the industry, and with the advent of WW2 all efforts were swept aside. Issues were raised again in the 1950s and in the interests of public health, actions were taken in the 1980s and continue today. These have been found to be effective in reducing consumption in the developed world, although high levels of smoking are still prevalent in poorer countries.

If using a product leads to a potentially fatal and unpleasant disease like lung cancer it is surely unconscionable to produce and sell it. The tobacco industry does not see it this way, considering the decision whether or not to smoke as a personal choice that people should be free to make. They resist all government health efforts to minimise smoking. When Australia brought in laws to require plain packaging for cigarettes the government was sued by tobacco companies (under USA law!) for taking action to reduce the sales of their product. In order to do this it needed to remove its corporate presence from Australia. It relocated to Hong Kong. The action failed in the courts but it illustrates the lengths to which some businesses are prepared to go to attack when anyone, including a sovereign, national government, gets in its way.

Removing competition.

The objective of competition in a capitalist economy is to encourage the development of products which provide a service to the customer which is better and/or cheaper than what is currently available. In this way, customers benefit from increasing value from products on the market. This competition is, of course, uncomfortable, with the arrival of a new predator into an existing, stable predator/prey environment. Existing companies can respond by upgrading their offerings. Alternatively, they can take action to destroy the competitor.

There are many tactics which can be used to this end. The law, itself, can be weaponised, as we discussed in Chapter 4. Patent law was developed to assist new product development. It can register a new innovation and award a patent which gives the patent-holder a monopoly over the patented innovation for a period long enough to reap the benefits of the new product, thus encouraging product development. Despite this noble intention ways can be found to subvert this law to the benefit of a company which holds a patent.

A story.

The following interesting anecdote tells such a story, occurring in the USA.

There are no generic versions of insulin available in the U.S.[13]

The reason for the current high cost of insulin in the USA is that today's insulin manufacturers do not have the same altruistic motives that drove Frederick Banting, Charles Best, and John Macleod—the inventors of insulin (or more specifically, the process for refining insulin from animal pancreases) — to sell their patent for $1 to the University of Toronto. They hoped that academic ownership of the patent would prevent drug manufacturers from engaging in the profiteering of a drug without which people with Type 1 diabetes would literally die.

As long as insulin was being made from animal pancreases this was a relatively effective tactic.

[13] This appeared in quora.com in September 2020.

But in the 1980s a large pharmaceutical company started selling an insulin produced by recombinant DNA — made by tricking e.coli bacteria into making human (not animal) insulin. Of course, very justifiably, they took out a patent — which in the U.S. gives the owner 20 years of exclusive control over the drug without competition from generics.

Naturally they could charge more for this new and better form of insulin. But at first the price difference was not that significant. People could still afford insulin.

By the early 2000s, though, that was changing. Insulin was about eight times as expensive (adjusting for inflation) as it had been 20 years earlier. Then the manufacturers realised that each new tweak in the formulation could get its own patent and be marketed at a higher price. And the new patent has a life of 20 years from the time of its granting.

As a consequence the price of insulin is about five times higher now than it was 15 years ago. In real dollars, that looks something like this: in 1985, a vial of insulin might cost $9–10. In 2005, it would cost $70–80. Today, it costs over $300.

In countries where drug manufacturers are producing and selling older (untweaked, but still very good) versions of insulin the price has remained affordable. In the U.S., typically the only form being produced and sold is the latest and most expensive version. Since they have no competition from generics or even older versions of insulin (which they conveniently no longer produce) they can get away with this.

There are many examples of gaming the system to undercut its efficient operation when 'business as normal' is threatened.

Chapter 6 – The Money Machine.

Positively malignant.

The human body is a wonderful example of a Self-Organising Critical System. Its immune system is a powerful and complex mechanism to protect against invasive bacteria and repair any damage caused. However, when the invader is cancer, it is not introducing an outside bacterium or virus. It is engineering a malfunction of the system itself. In fact it is a system operating with unrestrained positive internal feedback in which an elegant set of protective checks and balances is over-ridden.

It is quite similar to the global monetary system. Which is why we will use it here as a metaphor.

Talking Systems.

So what is a system?

A system is a group of 'things' and information flows which work together. A system may be:

Natural – a forest;

Socio-technical – a human-made system, such as a public transport system which is primarily technological but incorporates people as operators and clients;

Societal – a system which comprises just people, such as an education system. They may use technological supports, but only as supports to the people.

Chapter 6 – The Money Machine.

Systems can be mixtures of these, such as a forestry management system. Human-made systems are created to achieve human goals. Natural systems accept human interaction, but are not created with humans in mind.

These systems operate – they are self-organising – because they use feedback for control. The system continually measures its output and compares it to what it should be doing. Where a difference is measured the information is fed back to change this internal operation. This 'feedback' can be negative – telling the system to slow down, or positive – telling it to speed up.

As we have noted, business is inherently amoral – neither moral nor immoral. But to stop it from moving into immoral or unconscionable behaviour, governments have set up systems of business laws and practices. These provide the necessary negative feedback loops to keep the system operating for the good of the community.

Are there other systems which operate with positive feedback but no negative, controlling, feedback? There are many. Cancer is one. Explosives are another. Wild-fires are another, when they develop into uncontrollable firestorms. We will use cancer as our model.

A too-familiar example.

What do we need in a system to sustain a system runaway through forward feedback? Looking at the example of the human body, during healthy life, there is a system which cleans up and disposes of body cells which are damaged or grow too old to be efficient. They are detected, identified and eliminated by bodily systems. When cancer occurs, the correction systems are put out of action. The cancer becomes a runaway growth of previously healthy body cells until, through sheer mass and system disruption, it immobilises the bodily organs, causing system failure and death.

So we see that cancer is an example of a system with control systems over-ridden and with runaway positive feedback, which eventually destroys itself, by killing its host. What is necessary to set up a situation? It needs:

A failure of restraining, negative-feedback controls.
Disabling the immune system in relation to the cancer such that the cancer cells become invisible to the system which is supposed to detect and destroy them.

A driving mechanism.
The normal bodily mechanism of creating new cells within the body is hijacked by the cancer cells to allow it to produce, rapidly and unchecked, new cancer cells.

A driving energy to fuel the growth.

The body's internal energy system is used by the cancer cells. They go further, for example, in creating new blood supply networks specifically feeding the cancer.

Although there are, of course, huge differences in detail, if these three things are in place there is the potential for positive feedback loops to form.

So how does the financial system meet these conditions?

The Global Financial System.

Control methods.

There are restraining mechanisms in place in national and international laws. The issue is that entities at the top end of businesses in the Global Financial Community are truly global. It is possible for them to manipulate their activities to take advantage of laws in different jurisdictions to minimise losses to their income streams through taxes, tariffs, etc. It is in the interests of some countries to provide business conditions to minimise such losses – tax havens – so, in the global community, such avenues are always available for exploitation.

This provides the opportunity for control system failure.

Money generation.

The financial system (banks, finance companies, stock exchange, insurance companies) are unique in the business community in that that have one, identical product – money. Their input is money, their processes generate more money, and their output is money. So their business processes, which generate money out of money, provide an internal mechanism which could support a positive feedback.

This provides the driving mechanism for exponential activity.

Driver.

The focus of such entities in the financial system is to maximise profits for their shareholders. There is no product being provided to investors but money. Making ever more is their only raison d'être.

So greed provides the driving energy for running out of control.

All of the requirements for the Socio-Technical, Self-Organising system to run at uncontrolled, exponential growth are clearly in place.

Money.

Money is a chameleon. It changes its appearances and its characteristics, depending on where and how it is used. In very small amounts, it can make a poor life survivable. A little more makes a survivable life comfortable. More yet, and it can be used in business to employ people, create assets and services, pay taxes. At this stage the money in use is related to the products that businesses create. There is a clear link between money and everything that goes into its use. A pub may take out a bank loan, but it sees this as facilitating the provision of hospitality to its customers.

A step up from here happens when a business moves from an asset creator to a money generator. A group of successful lawyers decides to invest their savings into an enterprise which will give them a greater financial return than the money market and to achieve this they buy a nursing home. They have no deep understanding of the operation of a nursing home but believe that they can buy a successful one which will give a higher financial return.

This is a critical point.

It is the point at which the system moves from serving one purpose to serving a completely different purpose:

- The business moves from a service orientation focused on its clients to a money-earning role focused on its investors.

- The body moves from new cell generation in a maintenance and repair role to cell generation supporting the growth of a cancer.

In both cases the system moves from a situation which is beneficial to the client to one which is beneficial to a different, and less benevolent, entity.

Here the money chameleon makes a change of its colours, as a disconnect has now formed between the technical skills of the business owners and the operation of the business they own. A commodification of the business emerges – one nameless doctor can be replaced by another nameless doctor. Business principles of cost cutting and pricing are implemented. The new owners may have done their homework but they will not have the same feeling for the provision of a nursing home service as those who created it. It is easy for the business to see financial return as what it is all about.

As enterprises grow to global proportions those with a strong background in the creation of assets (automotive industry, pharmaceuticals, large-scale mining) the money chameleon changes to a darker colour. The creation of their products consumes large amounts of money, implementing science and technology to the service of the community, which is a highly valued activity. It is their raison d'être. However, within a global marketplace they also earn prodigious amounts of money. With the amounts flowing through their operation, they also become money-focused, seeking out means for tax minimisation, global investment, elimination of competition, and interference in national governments to obtain favourable operating conditions. It is in this realm that we find most of the world's billionaires. Typically, through luck or inheritance, along with a highly desirable and unique product and a single-minded approach to making money, these people can be among a handful of owners of businesses with enormous profits and cash flows, much of it ending in their pockets.

Is there a level above this? Yes there is; the money-machines. Their input is money, their output is money, and their business is maximising the difference between these two. The chameleon is now jet black. Here money is the income, the product and the reward. With single-minded dedication to this one task and with very large amounts of it to play with, this is a field where we will find many millionaires (CEOs and senior management with salaries and benefits in the multi-millions). Their activities support customers at a level higher still, namely the world's extremely rich. One often hears comments that 1% of the world's population now owns more than half the world's wealth. Oxfam reported another telling figure in 2014, stating that 85 individual people own more than the poorest half of the world's population. At this level the personal purchasing power of money can become irrelevant. Even the purchase of a private island with a holiday mansion, an airstrip and a corporate jet to whisk its owners away on holiday, will make barely a ripple in their money flows.

The driving force is simply an all-consuming addiction to money. Greed.

There are many ways in which the global financial system could be subject to distortion, but we will focus on one which is measurable – the level of financial inequality in a society[14]. Some level of inequality can be expected in any economy, and at relatively low levels it is probably a good thing as a reward to enterprise. Over recent decades the low end of the distribution of money, i.e., wages, has changed very little. Nevertheless, the level of inequality has grown exponentially because of huge increases in profit, flowing into returns to investors and into executive remuneration. This growth would appear to be far more than needed to encourage and reward business activity.

The USA demands that very large companies publish the ratio of senior executive pay to the pay of their median employee. Typical figures are around 400 times, with some going to 800 times and outliers much higher still so that a CEO can earn by lunch-time as much money as takes a year to earn for the average employee. Beyond the fact that is it clearly unfair, it also has damaging consequences for national economies and democracy itself, as we discuss below.

[14] There is a large amount of literature on the issue of inequality. One with a healthy mix of economics, reality and experience is Leigh, A, 'Battlers and Billionaires' Redback 2013

Chapter 6 – The Money Machine.

It appears to be unconscionable (depending on your conscience!) But, is it illegal? This implies that it contravenes laws. But which laws? Globalisation means that organisations can pick and choose between countries to find those with laws that suit them, and what international laws exist are usually poorly policed and carry few enforceable sanctions. The question of legality dissolves into meaninglessness.

If we recognise that the global financial system is a Self Organising Critical System we know how it can be expected to behave. We know that:

- It requires and must have in place negative feedback loops if it is to be controlled.

- It has inherent within it the potential for catastrophic runaway behaviour if positive feedback loops are allowed to exist.

When presented with these bald facts, proof of either extraordinary greed or an uncomfortable disregard for 'the common person on the street', governments are starting to make disapproving noises. Why else would the USA have made the requirement for companies to report the gap between executives and median pay rates?

Controlling the disease.

In the case of cancer, there is no question of holding back on possible treatments if they are effective. There can be no restraint or half-measures, no avoiding truth and no 'alternative facts'. Unfortunately, this is not true of the money system, where the power of big money makes it possible for protagonists to defy the application of effective 'treatments'. In fact, if the runaway behaviour of the global financial system is the cancer, then 'treatment' will be seen as a threat!

We are only taking cancer as a metaphor, using some features of cancers and their treatment to shine a light through a different window onto the operation of the global money market. So let's draw some parallels with three aspects of cancer treatment.

Radical surgery. Many cancers are confined to one body part. If the cancer is found while still confined to this part, and if the body can do without it, then the part containing the cancer can be removed. Examples would be breast or prostate cancer. This radical surgery proceeds on the basis that, although it will have undesirable side effects, patients will accept these when the alternative is death.

Chemotherapy. Some blood-borne or lymph-borne cancers grow and spread quickly. They are, however, in many cases, susceptible to attack with chemical agents, cytotoxins. The treatment relies on killing off the cancer cells and, while healthy cells are also attacked, there will be enough which will survive the cytotoxic flood to rebuild later into healthy body tissue. The treatment is unpleasant for the patient but again, is preferable to the alternative.

Radiotherapy. Often used to clean up after chemotherapy or when the type of cancer is not highly sensitive to chemotherapy. Radiotherapy is a heavy tool to use. It damages healthy tissue, relying on the body's ability in self-repair to rebuild healthy tissue in treated areas.

Controlling the global financial system.

How do these treatments of the cancer system shed light upon the financial system of the world?

We know that, if the global financial system should run out of control it would create an exponential growth in financial inequality in a population, primarily by rapidly producing more money, the vast majority of which would flow to the top few percent of the population. We know that there must be:

Control system failure.

For cancer, a failure of the immune system to recognise the cancer cells.

For the GFS, a failure of the laws created to provide negative feedback control.

If we find that a particular activity is hiding a negative feedback control loop from an out-of-control situation, we may look to radical surgery for a solution. If we find for example that money laundering is hiding money flows from restraint or taxation, we may attack the money laundering world with the aim of cutting it out of the body global.

A driving mechanism for the failure activity.

For cancer, an unrestricted generation of new cancer cells, as the immune system fails to recognise and destroy faulty cells.

For the GFS, internal processes which generate money from money in almost limitless amounts.

If the problem is tax dodging, we may use something like chemotherapy to attack mechanisms used here such as tax havens or complexity of international laws. We may again look to chemotherapy to provide adequate resources to find and prosecute these activities.

Driving energy.

For cancer, the cancerous cells co-opt healthy body activities for supporting cell growth, including building blood supplies dedicated to the cancer cell growth.

Chapter 6 – The Money Machine.

For the GFS, greed, the desire to acquire ever greater – limitless – amounts of money provides the driving energy.

The cancer cells are not strangers to the environment of the body. They are simply normal cells which have gone feral. The cancer co-opts normal, healthy body functions for its own needs and makes it very difficult to cut these off. The curative approach is to target the cancer cells themselves, so that, with their elimination, the body can carry out its normal functions in support of normal life.

For the global financial system the driving energy is greed. As has been observed[15] already, 'the love of money is the root of all evil'. Greed is an internal, human characteristic. Morals and ethical behaviour exist to help control this characteristic. However, it is a system at odds with itself through conflict of interest. It is difficult to control with laws alone. It requires a high standard of ethics in the governing of the countries of the world, as immoral players will always be able to find loopholes and methods for gaming any man-made system.

We come back to the point of needing leaders of great wisdom and morality. Plato would applaud, but would probably acknowledge that such leaders are rather thin on the ground.

---

[15] In the New Testament of the Bible, 2,000 years ago, and many times since.

Chapter 7 – Media.

Think of the press as a great keyboard on which the government can play.[16]

With the establishment of Parliament the British saw their country as comprising three estates, the Lords Spiritual (the church), the Lords Temporal (the aristocracy) and the Commons (the house of the people). With the opening of the houses of parliament to reporting by the press in 1787, Edmund Burke was moved to say, 'there are Three Estates in Parliament; but, in the Reporters' Gallery yonder, there sat a Fourth Estate more important far than they all.'

In its heyday, during the 19th century, England had become the centre of development of democracy as we understand it and the Fourth Estate grew to become an essential institution of this democracy. There was a sufficient news-hungry population to support many newspapers in a competitive environment. Called variously 'the papers' and then 'the press' it held sway over both those making the news and those reading about it.

The role adopted by the press became, in effect, the conscience of the government. The press was able to investigate issues in depth, examine their effects and implications, and broadcast their findings across the nation. It could, and did, call out unconscionable behaviour in government, in industry and in organisations and institutions of all sizes.

---

[16] Josef Goebbels, Nazi Minister for Propaganda

Part of the power of the press rested in the culture of the time. Personal honour was important and if a person's honour was seen to be damaged by their actions there was pressure for them to accept the consequences such as standing down from a role. The culture was reinforced by the religious climate of the time. Society operated within a publicly Christian framework and honourable behaviour was judged in terms of the commandments of the Bible – Old and New Testaments. Democracy was also taken seriously and the checks and balances placed by the press on the parliament and the operation of other institutions were seen as the operation of a state conscience, calling out actions which could threaten the operation of the democracy such as corruption, nepotism, conflict of interest, abuse of power and interference with the voting system.

How the world has changed!

In 2017 Wikipedia's 'Word of the Year' was Fake News.

In the context for doing 'good' religion has been abandoned. In a secular, scientific world the need to recognise a superior being appears to be superfluous. So we have abandoned Jesus' first command. However his second command could still serve a useful purpose in defining 'good', but this has undergone a not-so-subtle change. Rather than 'treat your neighbours as you would have them treat you', we have moved to something like 'treat the populace as the fools they are but make them think you are acting in their interests.' We use the full force of science and research into behaviour to achieve these ends. It is illuminating that much of the science we call upon to achieve this was originally developed for use by the military.

The 20th century has turned the media environment on its head. In this new environment, what sort of unconscionable things can the media be used for?

- Propaganda. Stories put out by governments to be read as truth by the populace to affect their group behaviour.

- Support of a political party, either government or opposition, and demonisation of their opposition.

- Distortion of the operation of the law

- Salacious raking over the details of gruesome crimes, naming names, continuing over years.

- Passing on, and giving increased credibility to unfounded rumours and conspiracy theories.

- Taking on long-running vendettas against people who offend or threaten them or their ideas and philosophies.

A global phenomenon.

Very rarely, perhaps once in a generation, the world produces individuals so unique that their effect on the world is dramatic and can set the course of history. Such a man is

Chapter 7 – Media.

Rupert Murdoch, the proprietor and driving force behind the News Ltd empire. Whether or not one approves of what he has done, and continues to do, there is no doubt that he has changed democracy and set it off on a new path.

He is called 'the king-maker' because his role in supporting this leader or that can make the difference between success and failure. A Conservative, a Republican, a Liberal – depending on what country he is in – Murdoch's view of the world is far right of right wing. It is said by former staff members and editors that he will stop at nothing to make sure of his candidate's success and, in return, his influence on that candidate will be assured.

Exerting the power of his media operations he has influenced such seismic events as:

- Britain's exit from the European Union (Brexit)[17].

- Britain's participation in the Iraq war[18].

- The election in the USA of President Donald Trump[19].

This kind of behaviour has changed the press and consequently changed political life in the USA, in Britain and in Australia. Through his direct influence on politics

---

[17] David Yelland, former editor of The Sun.

[18] Andrew Neil, former editor of the Sunday Times.

[19] Ken Auletta, of the New Yorker, referring to the use of Fox News.

and the lessons he has taught to other media operations one cannot discuss today's version of democracy without taking note of the king maker.

So where are we today?

All of these activities form part of every-day behaviour on the part of the news media and there are those who say that everything the Murdoch Press did, and does, can be paralleled by most of the other media. Perhaps we should ask ourselves if they really are unconscionable. They are driven by the need to sell content and people subscribe to the media to read, hear and see the content. If we were so bold as to submit them to the golden rule, 'do to others as you would like them to do to you', we would probably judge them as unconscionable. The press calls on voyeurism and schadenfreude. Do we criticise the activity or ditch the command?

If you eliminate God you also remove the threat of judgement in an after-life. The painful effects of an adverse judgement so picturesquely detailed in Dante's Divine Comedy are seen as no more than fairy tales, providing no restrictions on behaviour in life.

In truth, whether behaviour is conscionable or unconscionable barely matters any more. We still have in place a system of law, under the control of parliament, and equipped with institutions for trial, judgement and policing. This is fortunate because at least 'legality' still exists. In a world where money, and its accumulation, has really replaced religion — or even the belief in good and bad for their own sake — there appears to be no limit to what could be done.

With the decline of the integrity of the media and the erosion of the purpose of the Fourth Estate there is no doubt that the conscience of the community has, indeed, been outsourced to the law. We have pointed out that the law is a poor substitute and with the powerful in the community able to manipulate it, it is even shakier. However, the situation is not entirely lost. There are still journalists — brave individuals — who respect their craft and their integrity. They still find media accepting and publishing their work, as publishers find that people want to read what these journalists have to say. There are still public service media organisations — the ABC, Al Jazeera, the BBC, PBS — which are able to publish work, especially investigative journalism, which private media companies eschew. These systems are under constant pressure and experience funding cuts, board stacking and direct interference which limits their capability.

Part of the power of the press as the Fourth Estate was to ensure that unconscionable behaviour was exposed to the light of day. It could be visualised as a lighthouse, shining its light into the shadowy corners and illuminating issues to investigate. Yet today it seems to have been superseded by the metaphor of a watchtower, of the kind seen on the old Berlin Wall, staffed with guards with binoculars and others with sniper rifles, and sending out its troops to find every last piece of dirt to be used on the pages of the papers. If diminution of the Fourth Estate role removes the need for political behaviour to be conscionable, the parliament moves towards being a machine for the transfer of wealth from the poor to the rich.

Chapter 8 – Democracy Under Threat.

An anecdote.

In a previous life I worked in aviation safety. Our work was a small contribution to the global activities which led to the current extraordinary achievement of fewer than one accident per million flights. This amounts to about one per two million hours and, as the biblical age of a human is three score years and ten — about 650,000 hours − it is clearly safer to be on board an aircraft than not!

The key to achieving this result was to recognise that the root cause of every aircraft accident was a human error. Often it was an error by the pilot, sometimes by maintenance and service people, occasionally by the aircraft designers. The high safety level was achieved by recognising this, minimising the number of errors and trapping any that occurred. In any actual case there were always many contributions on the way from the error to the accident but the root human error was always there.

In writing this book it has become clear that a similar situation exists when we are look at threats to democracy. It is the thesis of this book that every threat to democracy has as its root cause an unconscionable behaviour. Again, in any specific instance there will be many contributions on the way from the original behaviour to the final, unfortunate result, but the root behaviour will always be there.

The idea is simple enough, although the mathematics to prove it comes from chaos theory[20].

Conscionability.

This is where we started out on our journey. We all have a conscience. Its core is in our DNA. It is based on ancient skills so innate that we hardly recognise them when we use them. When faced with an emergency our flight-or-fight reflex springs into action with no conscious willing from us. These are survival skills — we are here because they helped us to survive. On top of these we have developed a further quiver of skills to allow us to live together cooperatively in large societies.

Above the hard-wired basic skills our conscience is a social construct. We start building it at birth as part of our family nurturing. It is exercised in early childhood, battered and tested during youth and schooling, and then exposed to the blowtorch of adult life. We emerge into adulthood with a conscience. We can see and understand the value of the command:

Treat others as you would want them to treat you.

And then we see what actually happens in the real world.

---

[20] Mark Buchanan, 'Ubiquity', Phoenix 2000 provides more on this topic.

We find that trying to live life by this standard is difficult. There are powerful forces acting against us. If trying to meet the standards of the culturally developed conscience seems to threaten our more basic needs, such as the need to put food on the table, it is the cultural part of the conscience that gives way.

So we suppress our conscience and do things which it would tell us are wrong. It may hurt the first time but if we have to keep suppressing, and we see our colleagues suppressing theirs, we get used to it. After a while the still, small voice diminishes until we can't hear it any more. Our unconscionable act joins the flood-tide of other unconscionable acts within which our society wades forward, swims and occasionally drowns.

Honour.

The honourable person acts according to his or her conscience — the full construct of ancient knowledge plus cultural overlays. If honourable people commit acts which are against their conscience they experience shame. If others point this out to them, their shame is increased. They will blush with shame! It has been said that one rarely sees a politician blush.

As such actions are contrary to the honourable person's code of behaviour, the feeling will be unpleasant and painful, a feeling of letting themselves down in their own eyes as well as in the eyes of others.

Returning for a moment to the aviation analogy, a key issue in safety is to recognise when a human error has been made so that corrective action can be started. In our study of conscience we can see that shame is the flag which signals that an unconscionable act has occurred. It provides an opportunity for corrective action.

Of course, if the previously honourable person has been forced into a position where they must crush their conscience and do something which is, in their eyes, dishonourable and if they are forced to do this over and over, then their shame reflex will also diminish to the point of invisibility.

Transparency.

In our discussion on the media we made the point that the investigative and news reporting activities of the media have a key role to play in the operation and maintenance of a democratic system of government. This is the role of the Fourth Estate, the policing of the action of government and business to ensure that laws are obeyed, dishonourable behaviour is exposed and shamed, and that unconscionable activities which some may wish to remain hidden are exposed.

Within a democracy it is reasonable for average citizens to expect that whatever action is taken by the government is taken on their behalf and is intended to make their life better and safer. It may be that some things cannot be made public, and in these cases citizens should be able to assume that the government is still acting fairly. This assumption is hard to sustain if the press uncovers unconscionable behaviour which should not be hidden.

Transparency implies the ability of the citizen, through the media, to be able to gain a full, clear and honest view into the activities of government. Transparency should also apply to business, again exposing unconscionable behaviour, so that, if necessary, the government, acting on behalf of the people, can prevent such behaviour by use of the law.

Aligning with our thesis that unconscionability is the first sign of democracy-damaging behaviour, the role of a free press is crucial in addressing such behaviour before it becomes endemic.

Ignorance.

Economics has been roundly (and justifiably) criticised for basing its modelling on humans who are rational, knowledgeable and selfish. This concept is so far from human nature that any modelling based on it must be questionable at best. Similarly, the concepts of democracy assume that voters will be intelligent and fully knowledgeable in the views and reputation of political candidates, fully aware of the philosophies and history of political parties and aware of the principles of democracy and the way it is supposed to work. In other words, they will understand enough to vote in representatives who will best implement democracy. Not many people fit this mould. Most of the population are not that interested in democracy, beyond the interests of their tribe.

On any complex topic most people gain their understanding first by thinking about the issue and then by discussing it with family, friends and colleagues. The majority will go no further and just adopt these beliefs. If their significant tribes have fixed opinions on whom to support politically, these will often be taken on, almost as tribal markers. Those who are more concerned will read on the topic, seek out experts and consult them or read their writings, seek out and digest different and contrary views and identify an area of learning which comes closest to their own feelings. At some point they will stop investigating and accept the views and teachings of their chosen experts.

Politicians recognise that their first task is to get elected. They can rely on the fact that most people will not have thought deeply on the issues in play and most will have a very sketchy idea of democracy in action. Most people will be accustomed to making important decisions on the basis of emotion and the stories told by advertising. So getting votes becomes just another campaign to be sold to the people and the tools of advertising and psychological manipulation are brought into play, often at considerable cost. Despite his comments on democracy being the best system, Churchill also commented that 'The best argument against democracy is a five-minute conversation with the average voter'.

It is tempting to criticise people when they are simply behaving like humans. When they vote they typically react more to persuasion and emotional appeal than behaving rationally and intelligently. It is also an occasion when they come closest to behaving in accord with their conscience. So they cannot be accused of unconscionable behaviour. Nevertheless, this leaves them open to bad behaviour by those seeking their vote. Because of the significance of the vote this encourages unconscionable behaviour on a large scale, especially by major political parties.

Ill-will.

There will always be within the community those who wish to defeat the gains promised by a well-run democracy. These will typically be dishonourable people, primarily from the rich and powerful tribe, because these people stand to lose most from a fairer distribution of national wealth, and because they have the power to achieve their goals.

Conscience Outsourced

A democracy should operate in such a way so as to encourage effort and innovation in increasing national wealth, while ensuring the distribution of the benefits of this wealth in an equitable (although not necessarily equal) way across the community. The collection of taxes and their use to build public infrastructure is one such important activity. While the entire nation reaps the benefits of this activity, the rich and powerful as a tribe are very averse to paying taxes. In a recent debate between two USA presidential candidates, one, Hillary Clinton, accused Donald Trump of paying no taxes. Trump's response was 'So that makes me clever!'

The greed-driven accumulation of wealth which we have already discussed uses taxation as one of its primary methodologies. It drives governments to reduce progressive tax scales so that the rates of tax paid by the rich are little more than (sometimes the same as) the poor. Even then the taxes they should pay can be avoided by many methods, with the able assistance of the accounting profession. Taxes are easily collected from the poor so the major burden of paying for national infrastructure falls on them. This is unconscionable and is an example of dishonourable behaviour being used to undermine the democratic system.

What to do about it.

If we are concerned with these apparent threats to our democracy, we need to be able to identify places where the dishonourable behaviours, which are the triggers for damage, are occurring. Some suggestions:

- Make dishonourable behaviour more difficult to engage in without being discovered. Make laws which make the 'unconscionable but not illegal' defence more difficult.

- Make dishonourable behaviour a threat to career progress. Politicians, and others in influential positions, found guilty should not be able to hold positions of responsibility.

- Support the press in investigative reporting. Make whistle-blower laws more supportive for the whistle-blowers.

- Bolster and build public broadcasting in its role in investigative journalism. Fund it adequately.

If democracy is to be protected, the action taken should be meaningful, determined and persistent. The present situation has been reached because it is not apparent that this is on governments' agendas.

Chapter 9 – Outsourcing.

Do we really outsource our conscience to our Parliament, and through that to the Law? We have found that not only do we do this, but democracy cannot work unless we do. There are things which we would like to happen but could never be done without the immense resources of institutions, money, skilled people and assets, which are held and controlled by parliament.

As we have seen, once we have handed over to Parliament something in which we believe deeply, we may feel that we no longer have any responsibility for it. We rely on Parliament, which we have elected, to implement our needs and desires, using the law to implement and police these as needed.

We have discussed the rocky path followed in a democracy from ideas and needs into the design and enactment of appropriate laws, and their implementation through the public service. Laws are designed to improve the operation of the country. If they are well conceived, it is important that they are also well implemented. If they are not, the intended good will not be achieved.

When we speak about outsourcing our conscience to the Parliament, we only consider outsourcing parts of it. We know that the conscience comprises both an ancient, survival component and a newer, culturally developed overlay. The ancient part is hard-wired and individual-focused and not available for outsourcing. The cultural part exists to adapt and develop behaviour to fit into and support the function of our society. This is the part which is available for outsourcing.

A protest movement which gathers in the street calling for the dismissal of the government has clearly not outsourced to the parliament the running of the country. If they had been happy they would have outsourced that aspect of their beliefs to the government and left them to get on with it.

The conscience is a big-picture instrument. It is concerned with the overall beliefs and behaviour of the individual in society. A fundamental requirement of any outsourcing, and specifically outsourcing of the conscience, is that we aim to achieve a result which is better than if we had retained it to ourselves. The protesting crowd on the street obviously do not believe that handing over the running of the country to the present government will lead to a better society. They have retained in their consciences the belief that there is a better way, and their demonstration is a display of these beliefs.

Doing it.

In outsourcing our conscience we are back in the position of the Parliament itself – the big picture view.

Conscience Outsourced

1. I decide whether or not my government is sufficiently honourable to be trusted to operate as a true democracy. This is the 'due diligence' step. Given the known behaviour of many 'democratic' governments, and their propensity to lie to get elected, one could be excused for losing interest. However, let's assume that this government appears to be reasonable.

2. I make my opinion known to my representatives in Parliament. I can be proactive – write to my MP, form or join groups with the same view and put joint views to our MPs. Or I can do nothing more than see what our political parties say, and vote for the one which appears most likely to agree with my view.

3. I vote for the parliamentary candidates who appear most likely to agree with my view. If my candidate gets elected, so far so good.

4. If my candidate does not get elected, go back to step 2.

5. If my candidates are elected and their party forms government I must monitor its behaviour. If it progresses to my liking, so far so good. If not, go back to 2.

Conclusion.

The conscience has evolved over millennia as a valuable and effective survival tool. Democratic systems of government have integrated this developed conscience within their structures so that they form a bedrock for the operation of the parliament and the law, and thence the nation.

There has been a breakdown in our trust in these systems, and this can be put in terms of a degradation of the national conscience. The national conscience itself is directly affected by the consciences of the individual people of the nation through the processes of democracy.

Fundamental to the successful operation of democracy are truth, honour and transparency. It is these that we presently see in decay. What to do about it? As Voltaire is reported to have said:

The safest course is to do nothing against one's conscience. With this secret, we can enjoy life and have no fear from death.